FORTY WHACKS

– –

A one-act play for middle or high school

by
John Glass

www.studentplays.org
john@studentplays.org

<u>Copyright information. Please read!</u>

☞ About Student Plays ☜

Student Plays consists of **John Glass, Jackie Jernigan,** and **Dominic Torres.** We are a group of playwrights and directors that have written scripts for elementary school through college. We are proud of the variety of ages that our scripts serve.

Student Plays has "creepy" plays, and we also have Latino-themed plays. These are scripts that focus on Latino youth and the Latino experience. Any school can perform a Latino-themed play: it just requires a general introduction and basic exposure to the Spanish language, something that most schools and students already have.

To learn more, visit www.studentplays.org, or to contact one of the playwrights directly, simply email us at john@studentplays.org.

<u>Characters</u>

MAX   Twenties or thirties. Kind. Deferring.

DIANA   Late twenties, early thirties. Aggressive. Ambitious.

JACK   Only Jack's *voice* is heard, in a conversation with Diana via speaker phone. It is a very small part, at the beginning of Scene Three. (This role could be doubled with the LIZZIE role.)

LIZZIE BORDEN   The character herself. Twenties or thirties. The role is extremely minimal and has no dialogue.

The time is the present, and the setting is the Lizzie Borden Bed and Breakfast, in Fall River, Massachusetts. It is October. The entire play takes place in the front room of the hotel, an old room with the décor from the 1890s. There is a hotel desk, with a computer, telephone, clipboard and various papers. A rack of keys is hanging on the wall behind the desk. A portrait of Lizzie Borden is hanging.

If possible, there is also a sofa and a few easy chairs, and other usual furnishings.

The appearance by Lizzie at the very end of all three scenes is extremely simple and brief. During these brief scenes, if possible, a single light will shine on Diana, accompanied by a long note of music, something deep and mysterious; Lizzie Borden will then enter far stage right or stage left, and observe Diana from afar. She is holding a candle or a lantern.

SCENE ONE

Before the lights go up, the following audio is heard:

On August 4, 1892, the parents of Lizzie Borden were brutally hatcheted to death in their home in Fall Spring, Massachusetts. The evidence gradually pointed to Lizzie as a suspect, and she eventually was forced to stand trial for the murders. The trial attracted national attention, and even generated worldwide interest. However, on the 20th of June, 1893, in a courtroom in New Bedford, Massachusetts, Lizzie was found not guilty. Nonetheless, the legend of Lizzie Borden has become part of Americana, and has been established as one of the most macabre tales of our national heritage.

It is early Friday afternoon, and MAX and Diana are behind the desk, talking. As they talk they are working. Throughout this scene DIANA looks at and points to the large wall behind the desk.

DIANA: Think about it, Max. We could even have News 8 out here! The biggest excavation in Massachusetts history!

MAX: Excavation?

DIANA: Excavation. Wall tear-down. Whatever.

MAX: Sheesh.

(Pause.)

DIANA: Listen. I know Dad was always against things like this.

MAX: *And* Mom.

DIANA: Okay, Mom too. Maybe. But just think of what it could do for business! 'And here we are, folks, the hidden bottle of prussic acid! Still intact with the little skull and crossbones label on the back!'

MAX: Come off it! The Bordens were killed with an axe.

DIANA: But what *if* Lizzie first tried to poison them with the acid? You know that her parents were sick!

MAX: They were sick because they ate five-day-old mutton broth!

DIANA: That was never proved!

MAX: Ohhhh! Would you stop?
        (Beat.)
Damn, Diana . . . how many of those books *did* you read?

DIANA: I don't know. Come on. I never hung out here like you used to. I had to educate myself somehow.

MAX: So, how many?

DIANA: Uh. Four?

MAX: What?? Four books?

DIANA: Yes. And Max . . .? There's so many new theories out there. So much new research. After all these years, we could finally see a re-opening of the case! "We are here, folks, live with Diana and Max—the new owners of the Borden Hotel!"
(Off his face. Beat.)
Okay, sorry, *Max and Diana*. Not *Diana and Max*. But look: it could be HUGE!

MAX: Stop.

DIANA: The prussic acid is that forgotten piece of evidence. I'd like to sort of capitalize on it.

MAX: Would you let it go, please?

DIANA: We could even put it on Twitter!

MAX: We are *not* putting this place on Twitter. It's bad enough that all those silly travel reporters are constantly out here.

DIANA: Okay. True. But we—

MAX: Did you have room 4 cleaned?

DIANA: I did, yes. Took care of it myself.

MAX: Okay. What about the toilet in room five?

DIANA: Uh, yeah. Ugghh. Done.

MAX: Okay.

> *(Pause. She collects herself. She slowly begins to experience a headache here, which gradually worsens.)*

DIANA: I just see so much potential here. The prussic acid theory could really give a jolt to our business. I'd like to try and make something out of it.

MAX: What about the paint job? You got your way on that, you know. And that's not going to be cheap!

DIANA: But look at how fresh the place is going to look!

MAX: *And* that TV commercial . . .

DIANA: Well . . .

MAX: Don't forget about the hotel discount thing you insisted on. I'm still not sure about *that* idea.

DIANA: *(Rubbing her head.)* I checked the books. Mom and Dad hadn't raised their prices in over eight years. You know how inflation works.

MAX: You really need to see a doctor about that.

DIANA: I am. I'm going on Monday.
  (Pause. She is in pain.)
Oh, Max. You have no idea. The intensity . . . ohhh . . .

MAX: Do you need anything?

DIANA: No. No, it's fine. I've already taken aspirin.

MAX: Sure don't look like it.
  (Beat.)
Look. I admit. You sort of know what you're doing. You've
had your own business before.

DIANA: Yeah. Look how that turned out.

MAX: It doesn't matter. You were successful. You did
well. You were just—just *unlucky.*

DIANA: Well . . . yeah.

MAX: I just want to make sure we're making wise
decisions here, Diana. I know that it's almost Halloween,
and business is good. But . . . I *need* this job. I need this
income.

DIANA: I understand. We both do.

MAX: And I'd like to continue the decency that Mom and Dad maintained for so long. But . . . well, we had an agreement. Right?

DIANA: Yeah. I know.

MAX: So . . .?

DIANA: I know. If it really makes you uncomfortable, then I'll drop the whole idea.

MAX: Thank you. That *was* what we agreed on, right?

DIANA: Yes. Sorry for pushing.

MAX: Well. I just want to make sure we understand each other.

DIANA: We do.

(*Pause. MAX begins working on the computer.*)

MAX: Okay. So let's see . . . Judy is here on Wednesday. Then you have the young guy coming in, right? The part-timer?

DIANA: Yes. William. I think his name is William. He's going to help Joanna in the gift shop too.
   (*Beat. She notices a box on the floor.*)
What's this box?

MAX: It was in the attic. Papers, old letters. It also has tax receipts that we need to look over. And some important coding and licensing stuff.

DIANA: Oh. Yeah. Good thinking.

MAX: There's a lot of other old papers in there I need to go through.

DIANA: Are you still heading up to Boston?

MAX: This afternoon.

DIANA: Getting the rest of your stuff?

MAX: Yep. Might go to the Cape with Jimmy and his wife. And some people are throwing me a good-bye party from the post office Saturday night. Ha – two months later.

DIANA: Enjoy yourself. I'll have everything covered here.

MAX: Cool.

DIANA: Max . . . ?

MAX: Yes?

> *(Pause. She looks directly at the wall. MAX remains busy, working.)*

DIANA: Aren't you at all curious? As to what might be inside that wall?

MAX: What I think . . . . is that Mom and Dad asked themselves that same question for the thirty years they were here. But you know what they would want us to do. Or *not* to do. If there really is a bottle of prussic acid stashed in there . . . then . . . well, I just don't know. Taking that out of the wall would be a complete spectacle. And Mom would never want us to do that. She's the reason it never happened.

DIANA: Mom developed more of an entrepreneurial spirit than you think.

MAX: Diana, how do you know? You weren't around her for almost five years!

DIANA: I talked to Mom off and on. We weren't exactly estranged.

MAX: I just think that a wall tear-down would be chaotic. We've already got so much going on here. I mean, what about that TV commercial? What station is that going to be on? The Chill Channel?

DIANA: Yes.

MAX: Lord. And the website! Do you *really* think it needs updating?

DIANA: Let me get back to you on that. This web guy told me he might be able to do it in exchange for a yearly pass for his grandparents. They apparently love this place.
> *(Beat.)*

Max, you have to admit. Wall tear-down or not, we can make this place into a *fine* business. Not just a *business.* Creepy things have become hip all of a sudden. Mom and Dad fell into a business rut, and I'd like to change that! Attendance is up—

MAX: It's Halloween. Attendance is always up. *(He looks at his paperwork, begins to exit.)*

DIANA: Well, isn't that a good thing?

MAX: Yes.

DIANA: Hell, it should be Halloween year-round!

MAX: Around here it is. And I don't think there's a person better suited for this job than you.

DIANA: Of course there isn't! And look: we can't deprive Lizzie of her time to shine!

MAX: Lord . . .

DIANA: Halloween weekend's going to be packed, right? We should create a sound system throughout the whole hotel! Rattle some chains in the middle of the night! Maybe a witch cackle!

MAX: We aren't doing that.

DIANA: Just an idea, just an idea.

MAX: Well, your ideas scare me. Alright, I've got to do the laundry. Answer the phone, will you?

DIANA: Of course.

(He exits. Diana moves to the wall area. Stage becomes dark except one single light on her. A deep chord or note accompanies this quick mini-scene. As she puts her hands to her temples, experiencing more pain, she produces a tape measure, and takes several measurements of the wall.)

*(**LIZZIE** slowly enters stage left, and silently watches her. She does not exit. The light and the music gradually fade, end of scene.)*

SCENE TWO

Monday morning, a few days later. As the lights go up,
MAX is talking on the phone.

MAX: Wow. You should be one of our platinum members
or something.
    (Laughs.)
I mean, thirteen consecutive years. Wow. Well, thanks for
the business. Yes, Joanna is still here, out in the gift shop. I
left the post office, and Diana moved back after being out
in Tulsa for five years. Yeah. I sure didn't think we'd ever
wind up owning the place. But here we are.
    (Pause. Enter DIANA, just waking up, very groggy.)
Okay. You are all set. Party of four, two rooms. Around
three p.m., October 25th. Great, thank you! Bye.
    (Hangs up. Begins working on the computer.)
Wow. Two old couples that live in Maine, and they still
drive down here every year.

DIANA: Oh.

MAX: What's going on?

DIANA: Nothing. Trying to wake up. You're in here early.
(She gets a cup of coffee, gradually wakes up.)

MAX : Diana, it's nine o' clock.

DIANA: Oh. Shoot, so it is. Wow. Uh, how was the Cape?

MAX: We didn't make it out there. Just stayed in Boston the whole time.

DIANA: Oh.

MAX: We went to a Sox playoff game, and I got the rest of my stuff. It was clammy. That's one thing I bet you didn't miss about New England when you were away.

DIANA: Clammy weather beats tornados anytime.

MAX: Well. Yeah, I guess it does.

DIANA: Did you see the hallway? The new paint?

MAX: Yes. Looks okay, I guess. That's probably not the best for your migraines, though, you know. Paint fumes in the house.

DIANA: Oh. I actually hadn't thought about that.

MAX: Are you still having them?

DIANA: Not as bad. But yes. The doctor gave me pills but they've done nothing.
　　　(Beat.)
But hey: here's the good news! Look at the reservation book.

MAX: I'm looking right at it. How on Earth are we doing all this business?

DIANA: Isn't it great? Reservations for December! I looked back at the old books, and I could never find any reservations made here during the week of Christmas.

MAX: Uh-huh. I wonder why.

DIANA: What are you saying?

MAX: Nothing, nothing.
    (Sees a paper on desk. Beat.)
Oh. Are those students still coming out here to film their little documentary?

DIANA: Yep. This weekend, I believe.

MAX: Hmmph. They're just going to be *outside*, right? Getting footage of the house and neighborhood?

DIANA: Yeah, that's all. They're just college students. It's just some small project for their film class.

MAX: Hmmph.

DIANA: Don't start all that. That thing could be on TV one day. Those kinds of things are good for us. TV brings exposure, and more exposure means more business.

MAX: Well. True. But it's not . . . it's not always about the money, Diana. That's all.

DIANA: But at some point it has to be.

(The telephone rings. DIANA answers as MAX works at computer.)

DIANA: Good morning, the Borden House.
(Pause.)
We are out on Route 13, just past the Oyster Club. Yes. Exactly. About a mile past the Oyster Club. Okay, you're welcome.
(Hangs up. Pause as she looks at paperwork.)
So how many checkouts do we have?

MAX: Uh, four. Judy comes in at eleven, and William will be here at twelve. We can put them on the checkouts when they arrive.

DIANA: Okay.

(Beat. MAX notices something on the computer.)

MAX: Um. Wow. You let the web guy put those old pictures up already? Of the Bordens?

DIANA: Oh. Yes. We did talk about that, didn't we?

MAX: We talked about it. But that's about it.

DIANA: I'm sorry. I forgot if you were okay with that or not. I just went ahead and told him to do it.

MAX: I noticed. I'm looking right at it.

DIANA: You don't like it? Honestly, I think it helps bring in more customers.

MAX: It just seems a little macabre.

DIANA: Max, the whole house is macabre! That's what we're all about!

MAX: But showing bloody photographs . . . as a way of advertising?

DIANA: It helps people visualize what happened here. Come on, it's advertising! People need to see what we're all about. They can't just rely on . . . *(Sarcastically)* . . 'when she saw what she had done, she gave her father forty-one.'

(Pause. MAX puts his head down, stressed.)

DIANA: All right . . . look, how about this? I'll take down the picture of the mother's body. You know, the really bloody one?

MAX: Thank you.

DIANA: But at least let me leave up the other one.

MAX: You mean the one of Mr. Borden sprawled out on the sofa? That's actually the goriest one.
　　　　(Pause.)

Why are you so eager to launch this business so quickly??
Why not go into things more gradually?

DIANA: We've been here for three months! Why not?

MAX: Is this about trying to keep your mind off . . . your
divorce? Or . . . getting your confidence back after your
business was wiped out?

DIANA: Huh? I got divorced over a year ago. What are
you talking about?

MAX: It just seems hasty. It just seems—

DIANA: Don't start bringing up my time in Tulsa and all
that. My past is not relevant here.

MAX: Are you sure?

(Pause.)

DIANA: Look. It's true that I *do* want us to have our own
path now, Max. I want the bed and breakfast to be run in
our direction.

MAX: We agreed on that when we inherited it.

DIANA: And yes, I know: I *did* lose everything when I
was in Tulsa. But Max, I was the same way with my
business there. Aggressive. Business savvy! I want to
succeed here!

(Pause. She gradually begins to experience a head ache here.)

MAX: Well. Just don't forget that there are two of us here.
(Pause as he thinks.)
I need you to understand this. Sometimes I get worried. Worried about those pictures on our site and what people might think. And I . . .

DIANA: You *what*?

MAX: I don't know! I'm just concerned that people will get the wrong idea about us! That we're losing our reputation as a respectable business.
(Off the anguish on her face.)
You okay?

DIANA: Yes, I'm fine. Max, what other ideas would people have? I mean, we're not a wedding chapel or a place to have birthday parties!
(Pause. More pain from the headache.)
I'll take down the picture, Max. We can compromise, can't we?

MAX: Yes. We can. But is there anything else you're working on that you want to let me in on?

DIANA: Well, no. Not really.

MAX: Not *really*? No *searching for prussic acid*?

DIANA: No!

MAX: What about that television commercial? What's that going to cost?

DIANA: It'll be cheap! I'll give you the details when I find out everything. I've forgotten the actual price. But it could really bring business, Max. Loads of it!

MAX: Whatever. What *is* the Chill Channel, anyway? Horror movies?

DIANA: Uh, yeah. Basically.

(He sighs, picks up a clipboard and turns to exit.)

MAX: All right, sis, let's communicate. Don't do anything else crazy without talking to me first. Let's don't screw up what we have here. I don't want to go back to working for the post office.

DIANA: Max?

MAX: What?

DIANA: You ever . . . do you ever have bad dreams?

MAX: Bad dreams? Nightmares? No.

DIANA: Oh.

MAX: Why?

DIANA: Just wondering. You know, I think about them sometimes.

MAX: It's those horror movies you watch.

DIANA: No, I haven't watched any of those lately. Seriously.

MAX: Well . . . I don't know. This place isn't messing with you, is it?

DIANA: No, of course not. Please.
    (Forces a fake laugh.)
I just have these crazy dreams sometimes.

MAX: Alright. Well. You gonna be okay?

DIANA: Yes. I'll be fine. Just need more rest.

MAX: Alright. I've got to go to the bank. Take your aspirin.

> *(Exits. The same single light and deep note of music accompany this mini-scene. Diana walks over to the wall, pulls out notepad and tape measure, checks one measurement on the wall, writes it down. She continues to experience the headache, then gradually resumes with the measurements.)*

*(**LIZZIE** walks out, as before, and silently observes Diana. She remains there until the light fades. End of scene.)*

SCENE THREE

A few days later. As the lights go up, DIANA is wiping the countertops/tables with a wet rag, working, speaking to JACK by speaker-phone.

DIANA: Yeah. I understand. Look, I just want to be sure that I won't be facing anything legal if I go through with this.

JACK: Well, that's what I was telling you. When Stanford Law School did a mock trial of the Lizzie Borden case in 1997, some people were concerned that was what might happen.

DIANA: So . . . what happened?

JACK: Well, it was just a mock trial at a university so basically *nothing* happened. And I don't think that it affected the bed and breakfast. But some members of the Borden family did issue a statement, claiming they weren't comfortable with it.

DIANA: Really?

JACK: Yes. Now . . . that was sixteen years ago. But think about it: what if you really *did* uncover an old bottle of prussic acid inside that wall? Is that what it's called? Prussic acid?

DIANA: Yes.

JACK: Okay, well, imagine if that really *is* in there. She supposedly tried to poison them with that, right?

DIANA: Yes.

JACK: Be careful of what you ask for. No matter what the speculation is, you know that the Bordens were killed by an axe, not by poison. What you're doing could ruffle some feathers somewhere. Your parents were the owners there for a long time. But remember, they weren't part of the Borden family. Neither are you. Rest assured, there are distant members of the Borden family out there somewhere.

DIANA: Yeah.

JACK: And also, Diana, you've got to remind yourself: Lizzie Borden was never found guilty. An excavation like that could be disastrous.

> *(Pause. Enter MAX, wearing rubber gloves and carrying a bucket.)*

DIANA: Or it could be successful.

JACK: Well, yeah, that too.

DIANA: I appreciate it, Jack. I always know who to call when it comes to this kind of stuff.

JACK: That it?

DIANA: *(Hurriedly, due to MAX.)* Yes. That's it. Gotta go.

JACK: Anytime, Diana. Take care. I'm glad you're back in New England.

DIANA: Thanks. Bye.

> *(Hangs up. Pause.)*

MAX: Who was that?

DIANA: Oh, nobody. Old college friend. He's a lawyer. I had to ask him something about my divorce. What are you doing?

MAX: It's those people in rooms seven and eight. You know, the goth group.

DIANA: Oh yeah. Interesting bunch.

MAX: 'Interesting' is putting it mildly. I just cleaned candle wax off the nightstands in both of their rooms.

DIANA: Candle wax?

MAX: They had candles all over the place in there. Looks like some kind of seance was going on.
> *(Pause.)*
You know them, right?

DIANA: Well, they're some friends of Keith. You remember Keith.

MAX: Yes. But, damn. They were here for three days. Did they use that weekday discount thing we ran a while back?

DIANA: Yes.

MAX: Figures.

> *(He goes to computer, works. DIANA's headache gradually begins again, and it escalates throughout the scene.)*

DIANA: Well, sorry. What do you want me to say? They're customers that took advantage of a travel coupon. I didn't ask them to light candles in the room.

MAX: They were also up all night last night. I heard them. I don't know how we didn't get any complaints.

DIANA: Well . . .
> *(Pause. The telephone rings, and she picks up.)*
Borden House, can I help you?
> *(Pause.)*
Oh, yes. Yeah, I'm sorry. We are booked Halloween night.
> *(Pause.)*
Yes, that's right! Sorry.
> *(Pause.)*
Okay. Thank you. Bye!
> *(Hangs up.)*

MAX: Diana . . . those pictures are still on the site.

DIANA: Oh. God. I totally forgot, Max.

MAX: You said you'd—

DIANA: I know, I know. I'll take care of it. I haven't been feeling very well.

MAX: Today?

DIANA: Huh?

MAX: Can you do it today?

DIANA: Max, we already have so much to do today.

MAX: I'd feel a lot better if they were off the website as soon as possible. I . . . *(Beat. Reading the screen.)* What's this email?
    (Pause as he reads.)
A reporter from the Eagle? What . . . ?

DIANA: Shit. He used the hotel email?

MAX: Yes.

DIANA: Sorry. He's supposed to email *me*. It's just a writer.

MAX: Huh?

DIANA: He wants to do a feature on us as the new owners.

MAX: Are you sure that's all he's interested in?

DIANA: Well, I don't think he's interested in *me*.

MAX: Don't be cute. That's not what I mean. He says here that 'he has a particular interest in the potential tear-down of the wall.' I'm looking right at it.

> *(Pause. She puts her hands to her head, in great pain here.)*

MAX: Those pictures on the web are one thing. And I'm not going to even bring up that ridiculous TV commercial. But—

DIANA: You just did.

MAX: What's going on around here, Diana? Everything is just—just—

DIANA: Just WHAT?

MAX: Everything's spiraling in a certain DIRECTION! That's what! Reporters! Séances!

DIANA: How do you know there was a séance in that room??

MAX: Why don't we talk about the wall? That's what I'm really concerned about! You lied to me. What the hell are you trying to pull?

DIANA: I'm not trying to pull anything!

MAX: We agreed that we weren't going to do a tear-down! You told me you were going to drop that whole prussic acid thing!

DIANA: It's just an email.

MAX: But you promised me that you weren't going to pursue that! And now a local newspaper knows about it??

DIANA: Why are you flipping out all of a sudden?

MAX: Because we are losing any sense of Mom and Dad's honorable ways! That's why!

DIANA: Please!

MAX: I know, Diana. About Tulsa.

(Pause. Heavy beat.)

DIANA: What?

MAX: I know about Tulsa. I know that you filed bankruptcy long before that tornado wiped your business out. I know.

(Pause.)

DIANA: Who told you?

MAX: I talked to Kevin. He called and . . . we started talking. It all came out.

DIANA: He called?

MAX: He called.

DIANA: What the hell did he want?

MAX: He needed some information, something about some tax papers from when you guys were married. It sounded important.

DIANA: Shit. He already has all that stuff.

MAX: I told him to email you. The point is he called, and we started talking. And it all came out.
   (Pause.)
And I think I'm beginning to connect the dots here.

DIANA: Whatever. What happened in Oklahoma has nothing to do with all of this.

MAX: Well, whatever it was, I don't even care. We're family. We'll move forward.

DIANA: Are you sure?

MAX: Yes, I'm sure! But I see the way you've been acting since you got back. And I'm really concerned that whatever happened out there is affecting you here!

DIANA: You can stop worrying because it's not!

MAX: But that's *exactly* what's happening! I know you. You're an overachiever. Your ambition . . . and pride. How this whole thing with the wall can bring the business more recognition, fame, and—

DIANA: I never said I *absolutely* wanted to go through with the excavation! All I did was contact that reporter!

MAX: Would it make you happier if we just went ahead and did it ourselves?

DIANA: What are you talking about?

MAX: Here! The tool box is right down here!
    (He furiously grabs it from under desk.)
Let's just get it out of the way. Forget about decency! About respect! Let's just make this place the lobby to hell!

DIANA: *(In enormous pain.)* No.

MAX: Come on! Why not? Your persistence has no end. You said so yourself!

DIANA: NO!!

MAX: I'm worn out by all of this, Diana!! Seriously!! Let's just DO IT!!

DIANA: I said NO!!

(She grabs the toolbox and slings it to the floor with a crash. Long pause. They catch their breath.)

MAX: Sorry. I . . . I shouldn't have.

(Pause. DIANA walks off, paces.)

DIANA: I . . . found some of Mom's old diaries and letters, Max. They were in that box from the attic.

(Pause.)

MAX: And . . . ?

DIANA: It's in there. In Mom's diaries. In her writing. You were right. I can't believe I'm actually admitting to this . . . but she would *never* want us to do this wall teardown. *They* would never want it. I've been trying to tell myself otherwise. But you were right.
(Pause.)
And I'm not so sure that *other* people would want us to do it either.

MAX: What are you saying?

DIANA: I'm asking you . . . if you can forgive me for being so bullheaded around here. So . . *hasty*, as you would say.

MAX: Well . . .

DIANA: I'll take those pictures down from the site. I'll drop the whole idea. The tear-down. Emailing that reporter. Everything. And I'll try to chill out.
　　　(Pause. Closes eyes, puts hands to temples.)
I think that my headaches . . . well, let's just say that the house may have something to do with them.

　　　(Telephone rings)

MAX: I'll get that.

DIANA: No, let me. I'm fine. I got it.
　　　(Picks up.)
Borden House?
　　　(Pause.)
Excuse me? Oh. Okay. Yes. Yes, ten o'clock. Right, it's on our calendar. We're all set. Thank you.
　　　(Hangs up. Pause.)
That was the termite guy. He'll be here Halloween morning. Ha—of all days.

MAX: Diana . . . are you okay?

DIANA: Yeah. I think I am. I really do.

MAX: Are you sure? I'm almost scared to ask . . .

DIANA: So don't then. Seriously, it's fine. I'm okay.
  (Pause. Takes a breath.)
Max, you are right. Our business is doing well. But I'm just
. . . over-anxious sometimes. I *do* let ambition get the best
of me. I have to admit: Tulsa really did a number on me.
You have no idea. And I believe maybe something *here* has
done a number on me as well. But I think it'll be fine.
  (Pause as she reflects.)
One day we'll talk about it. But for now, this wall needs to
stay the way that it is.

MAX: Do you really think there's a bottle of prussic acid
somewhere in that wall?

DIANA: A lot of people certainly think so. The so-called
Lizzie Borden scholars. But as for me . . . I don't think I
want to know.
  (Pause. She rubs her head.)
I don't think I *ever* want to know.

  (He goes to pick up the tools.)

DIANA: No, I'll take care of that. Can you . . . give me a
minute here alone, Max?

MAX: Yeah. I guess so.

DIANA: Can you get those towels for room nine? Please?

MAX: *You're sure you're okay?*

DIANA: I'm fine. *(Pause.)* I'm fine.

MAX: *(Begins to exit.)* Okay.

DIANA: Hey . . .

MAX: Yeah?

DIANA: Mom and Dad's honorable ways, huh?

(Pause.)

MAX: That's right. Mom and Dad's honorable ways. Even in the Lizzie Borden house.

(He exits. She pauses for a moment, putting her fingertips to her forehead, relaxing. She walks to the wall, touches it with one hand, deep in thought.

(LIZZIE enters far stage left or right, one final time, and observes. When DIANA turns and slowly walks over to pick up the tools, LIZZIE exits. Lights fade. End of play.)

✎ Alternate ending ✎

This is an option for the very end of the play. It simply replaces the stage directions above that begin with "He exits."

He exits. DIANA pauses for a moment, putting her fingertips to her forehead, relaxing. She walks to the wall, touches it with one hand, deep in thought.

Suddenly, DIANA swiftly turns and marches to the tool box, picks up a large hammer or hatchet. Long pause as DIANA holds the tool and focuses on it. LIZZIE enters far stage left or right, one final time, and observes. DIANA slowly turns and walks toward the wall, still holding the tool. LIZZIE begins to walk toward DIANA, without her knowing it. The lights slowly fade. The long note is heard as the lights fade. End of play.

☞ **More from Student Plays** ☜

Othello's Just Another Fellow

Dramedy. **Grades 5-7.** 25-35 minutes. 8 actors: 4 males, 3 females, one teacher (or student portraying a teacher) 3 to 5 extras, if needed. ****A Latino-themed play****

A group of students are involved in a school production of *Othello*, but one of them is disturbed about the lack of diversity in the play. He takes certain steps to disrupt the play but in the end is encouraged by the others to try and make a difference in another, more constructive way. A lesson is learned, and the production is saved from disaster!

Pagasqueeny's Pantry

Comedy. **Middle/High School.** 15-20 minutes. 6 actors: 3 females, 2 males. One student (or a teacher) plays the comical role of the elderly Mr. Pagasqueeny.

Three friends sneak into Mr. Pagasqueeny's home to get something that one of them left behind. But in walks Pagasqueeny and they must hide in the pantry! In this comical play, a lesson is learned about honesty and trust, but it takes a heated discussion in the pantry and a subsequent attempt to escape to find this out!

Una Carta de Abuelo

Dramedy. **Middle/High School.** 35-45 minutes. 10 actors: 1 teacher, 5 females, 4 males. (With the option of 4-5 extra actors in two scenes.)   ****A Latino-themed play****

Two cousins discover an old letter in their late grandfather's comic collection that they think leads to treasure! The cousins often butt heads, with one believing that he is more "Mexican," the other believing that some people make too much of a fuss about "being Mexican." Thus, they form their *own* groups in search of what Grandpa hid long ago. But what they find is actually worth more than merely silver or gold.

Barbecue at the Prom!

Dramedy. **Grades 5-8.** 25-35 minutes. 6 actors: 3 females, 3 males

It's a classic tale of guys versus girls! It's a prom committee, and everybody is supposed to work together but differences and opinions get in the way, causing the guys and girls to form their groups. For the end-of-the-year prom, one side wants pasta and lace, the other wants sports and barbecue! The two groups square off but eventually work together, demonstrating the importance of cooperation and compromise.

Going to Guatemala

Dramedy. **High School.** 50-60 minutes. 11 actors. 6 males, 5 females.   ****A Latino-themed play****

A Latino student is chosen at the last minute to join a humanitarian group from his school that is headed to Guatemala. But since his Spanish is weak, he faces ridicule and criticism from certain peers. Jealousy and anger trickle throughout the campus as the trip approaches, and the social buzz of the high school becomes even more hectic when the student's trip money is stolen on campus, jeopardizing his trip.

Stravinsky's Kitchen

Comedy. **High School/College.** 12-15 minutes. 3 actors: 3 males (or females).

Two friends secretly enter the home of an employer to obtain a forgotten object but the homeowner abruptly arrives home while they are there. As they hide in the kitchen's pantry and plot their getaway, the two talk and eventually argue, exposing the true colors of one of them. Upon their hasty exit a mistake is made, and one of them capitalizes on this mistake, resulting in his/her fortune.

Forty Whacks

Drama. Spooky. **High School/College.** 25-35 minutes. 3 actors: 2 females, 1 male.

A pair of siblings have inherited the Lizzie Borden Bed and Breakfast in New England. Although the business was run for decades in a quiet, respectable fashion, one of the siblings is over-ambitious, wanting to unearth an alleged piece of buried evidence within the house. This brings about a chilly uneasiness between brother and sister, and perhaps within the house itself.

John Calhoun and a Thief

Drama. **College.** 35-40 minutes. 3 actors: 2 females, 1 male.

Kicked out of a university PhD program, a bitter and dejected female lifts from the library archives original copies of John Calhoun's personal documents. Counseled and consoled by her roommates, her conscience slowly gets to her; but as she seeks entry to other universities her luck turns to worse, and the subsequent decisions she makes regarding the historic papers cause this one-act play to become darker, if not funnier.

Honoring the Hijacker

Drama. **College.** 12-15 minutes. 4 actors: 2 females, 2 males.

It's 1981, the ten-year anniversary of the famed hijacker D.B. Cooper. The play's four characters are attending a "D.B. Festival" and have stayed up very late, outlasting everybody else. The late night chit-chat goes from pranks and jokes to outright volatility, and suddenly this get-together becomes something that three of the four characters didn't bargain for.

It's a Super Day at Sammy's!

Comedy. **Middle or High School.** 35-40 minutes. 9 actors: 5 females, 4 males (4 possible adults).

Jodi has found a summer job at a travel agency. But her three younger siblings can't seem to live without her! They call her at the office incessantly, which interferes with the work. The standard telephone greeting "It's a super day at Sammy's!" becomes a repeated theme of this comedy, as Jodi struggles to reach a balance between her job and her nagging siblings

Three Tenners

Comedy/Drama. **Elementary through High School.** Three Ten-Minute Plays.

Three Creepy Plays

Drama. **Middle School through College.** Three short 'creepy' plays.

Hockey Masks in Hueytown

Drama. Spooky. **High School/College.** 20-25 minutes. 4 actors: 2 males, 2 females.

Driving home for Thanksgiving break, four college students stop off in a small rural town to retrieve one of the student's old family pictures. They reluctantly enter the empty home of his deceased uncle, a former producer for the Friday the 13th movies. Strange objects are found during their search . . but when a hockey mask surfaces, everything really goes sideways.

The Witch Makes Five

Drama. Spooky. **High School.** 10 minutes. 4 actors: 2 males, 2 females.

After a bizarre group camping trip, a student is checked into a youth mental facility . When she is visited by the other members of the trip, memories of the weekend trickle out . . . and horrific things begin to happen.

Mrs. Calapooza and the Culebra

Dramedy. **Grades 5-8.** 10 minutes. 5 actors: 3 females, 2 males.

Fed up with their grouchy teacher's classroom ways, four students complain and bicker back and forth during a Spanish quiz. The situation grows worse when the friends discover that one of them has pulled the ultimate prank on the teacher.

Raiders of the Lost Rakasa

Dramedy. **Grades 5-8.** 10 minutes. 7 actors: 4 females, 3 males.

Seven young explorers arrive at a cave in a far-off land in search of the great "Rakasa." They find what they want . . . along with a few of the cave's unexpected surprises.